The Wild "Up North"

A coloring book for everyone.

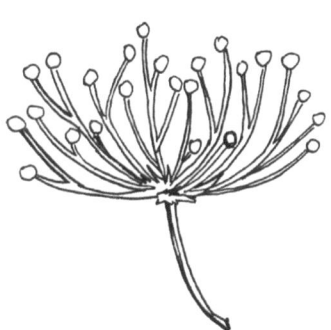

By: Sarah Putnam

Copyright © 2020 by Sarah J Putnam
All rights reserved. This book or any portion thereof
may not be reproduced or used in any manner whatsoever
without the express written permission of the publisher
except for the use of brief quotations in a book review.

Printed in the United States of America

First Printing, 2020

ISBN 9798563347342

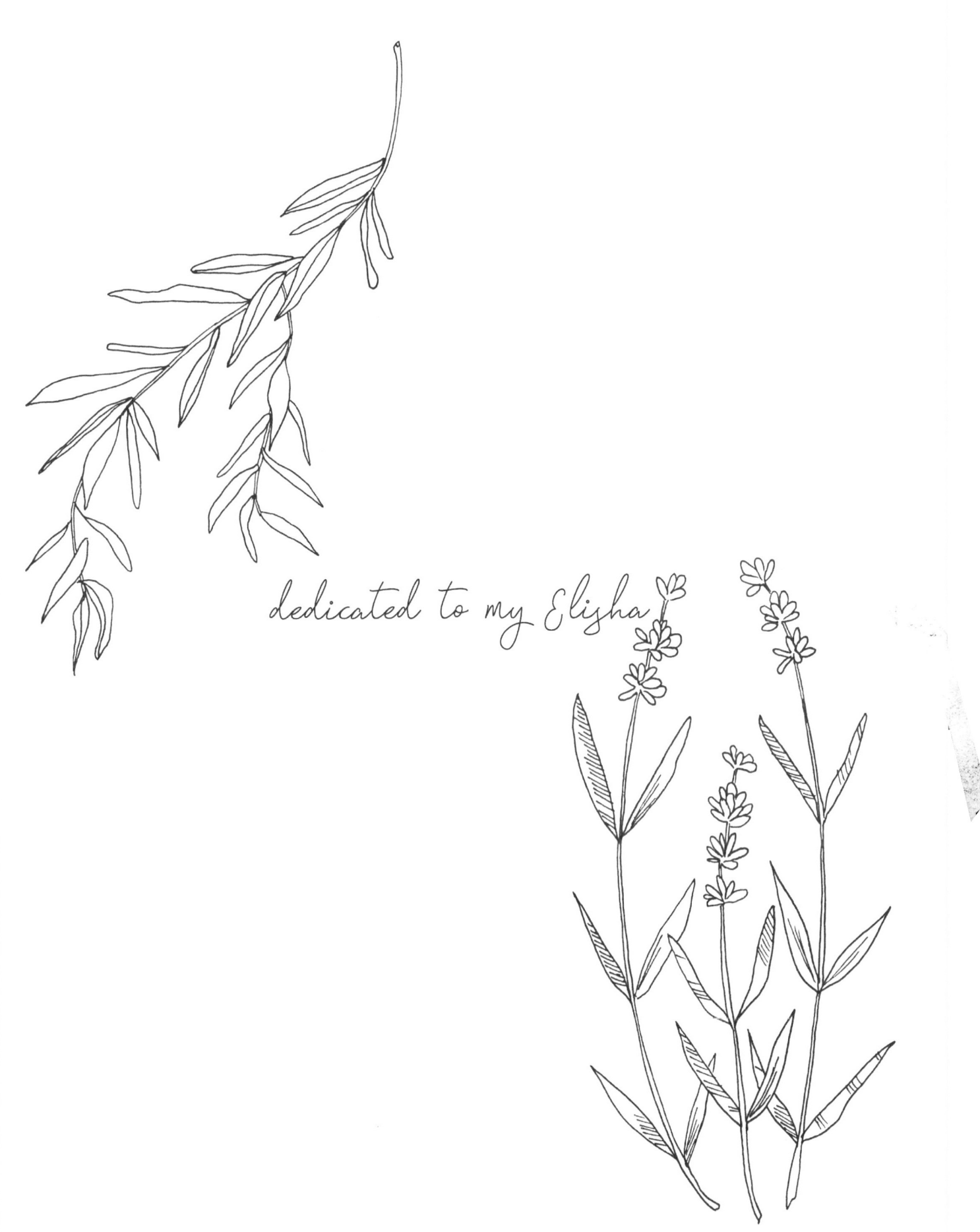

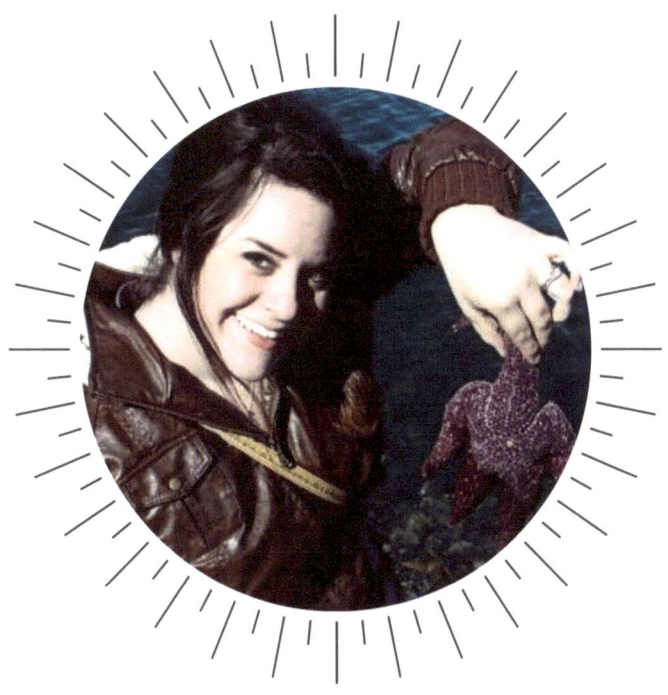

A Note From The Artist

From growing up in small-town Wisconsin to living an adventure in Alaska for five years and now finding new sights in Michigan, I have experienced a good share of wild beauties and WONDROUS landscapes "Up North."

My hopes for you are that you'll venture out and find your own beauty, wherever that may be! The world is full of crazy, wild, colorful wonders! In the meantime (and all the in-betweens of your adventuring) I hope you enjoy every moment spent coloring the beautiful wilds in this book.

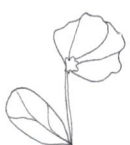

Sarah Putnam

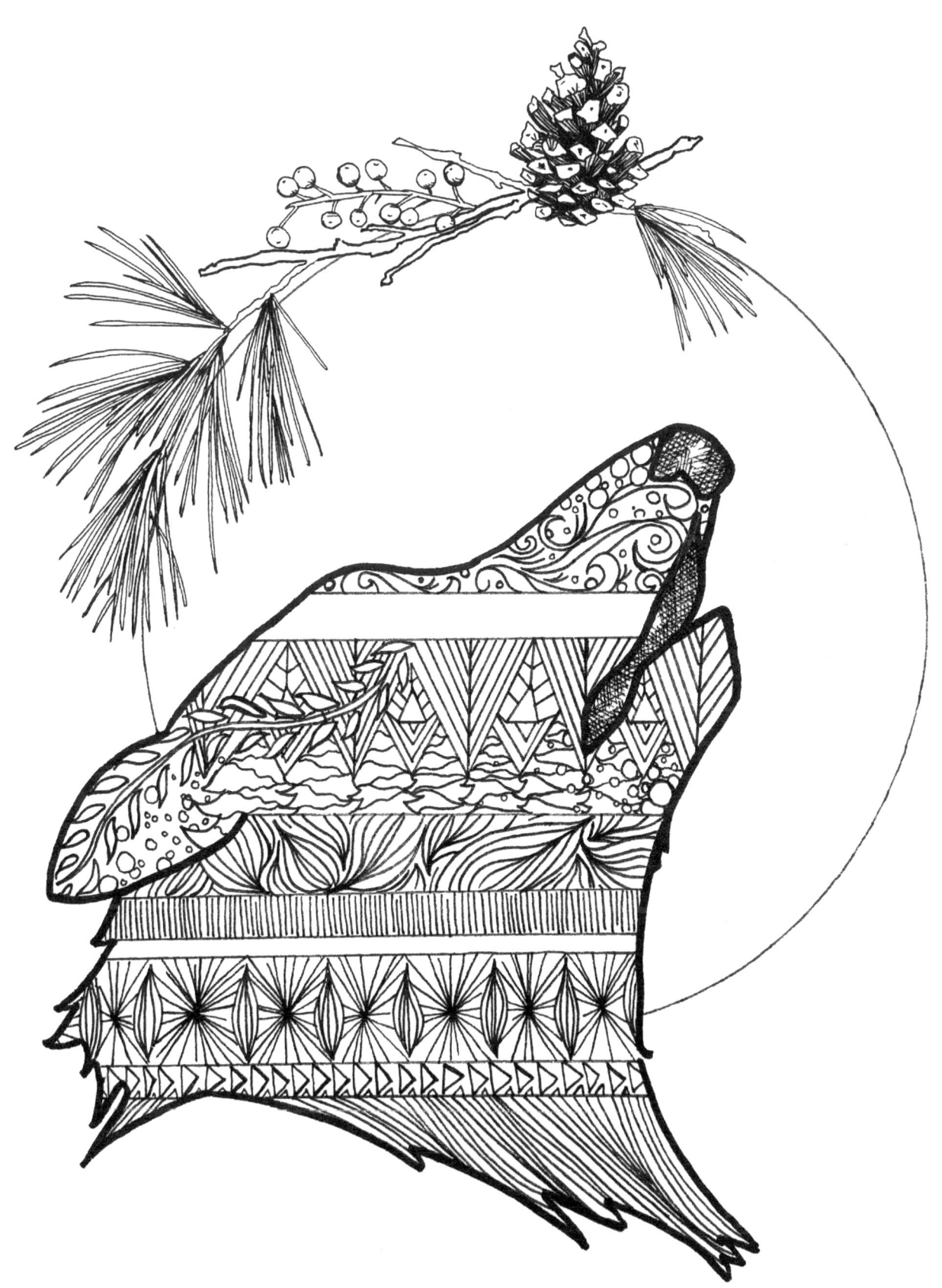

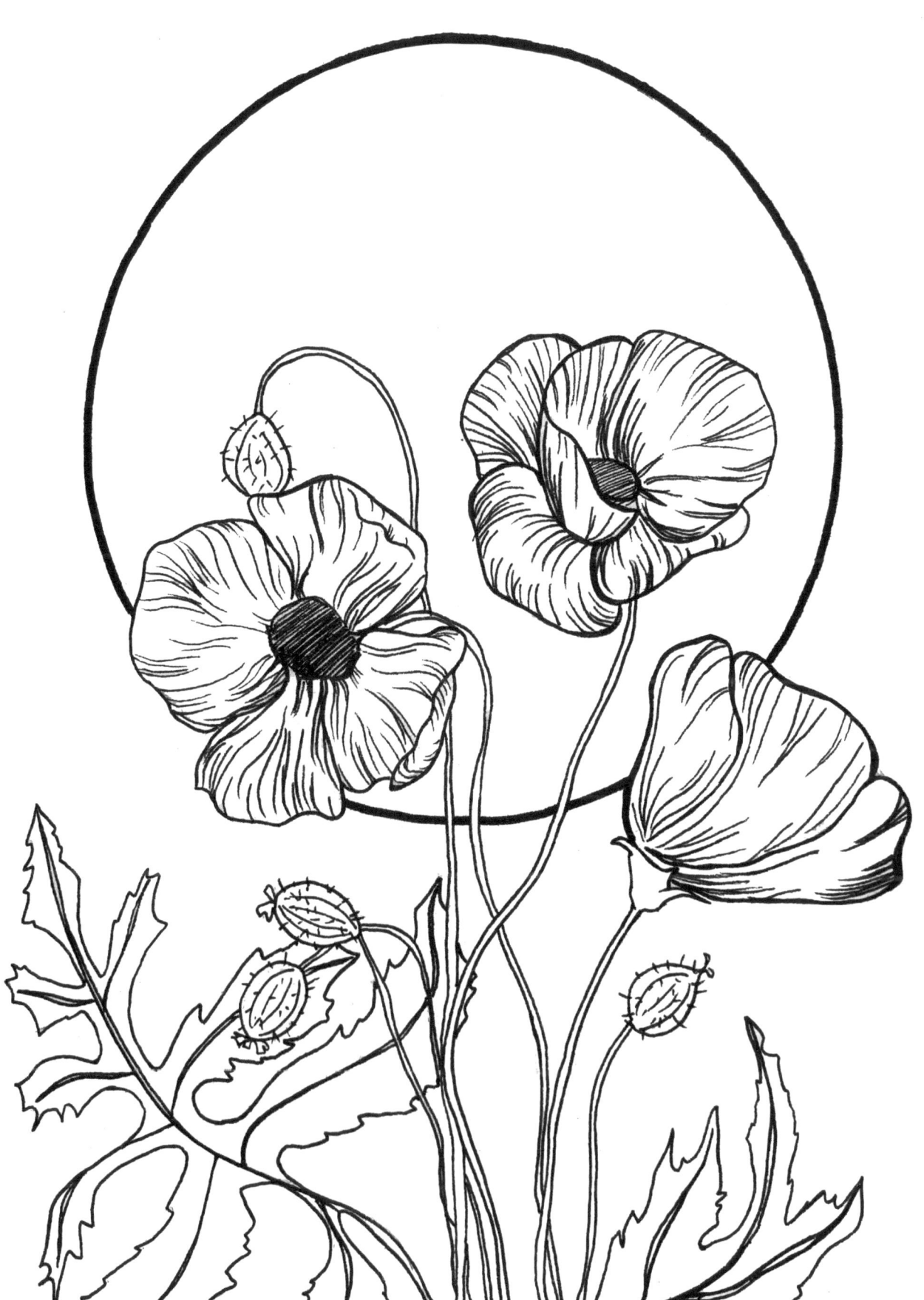

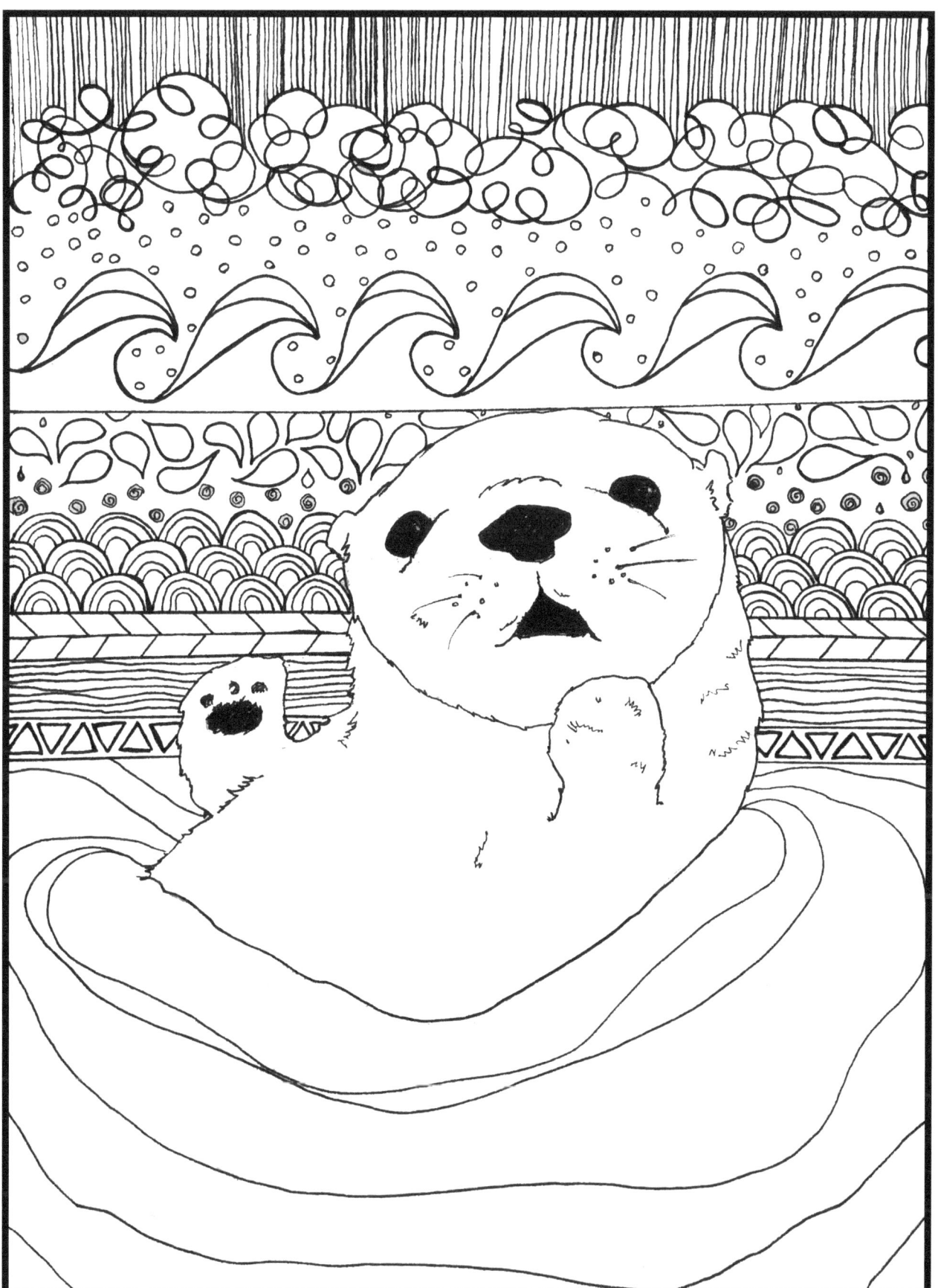

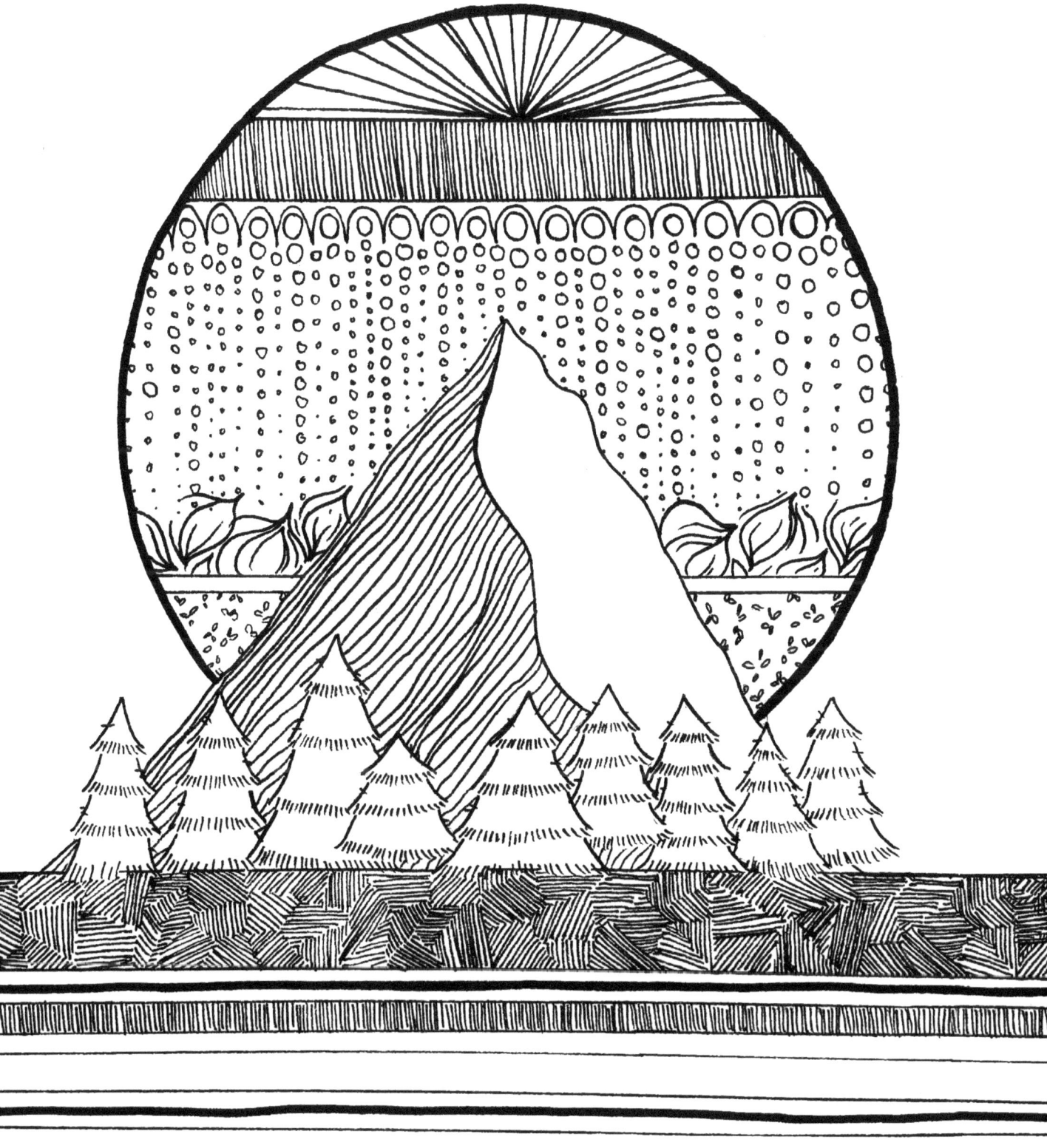

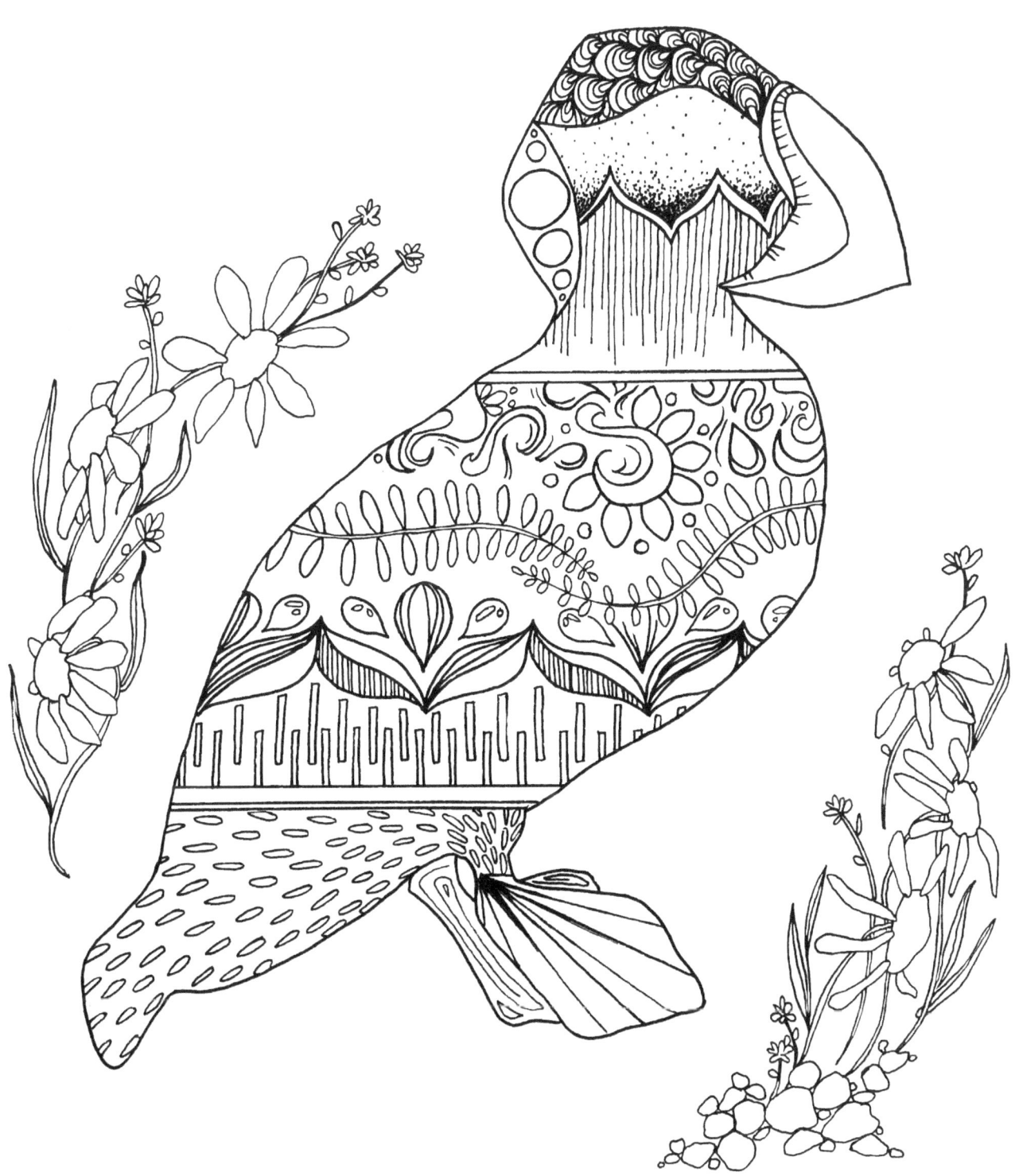

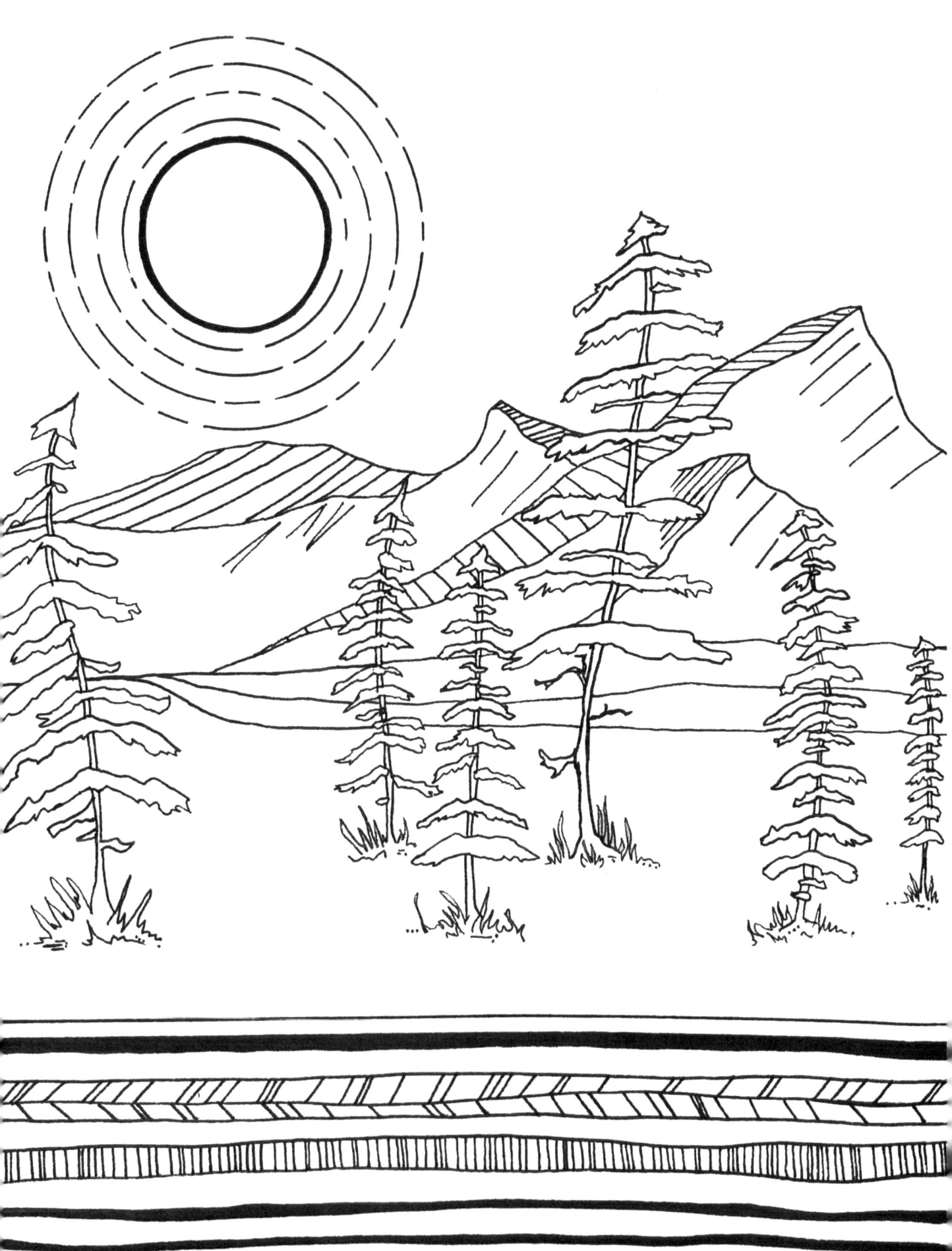

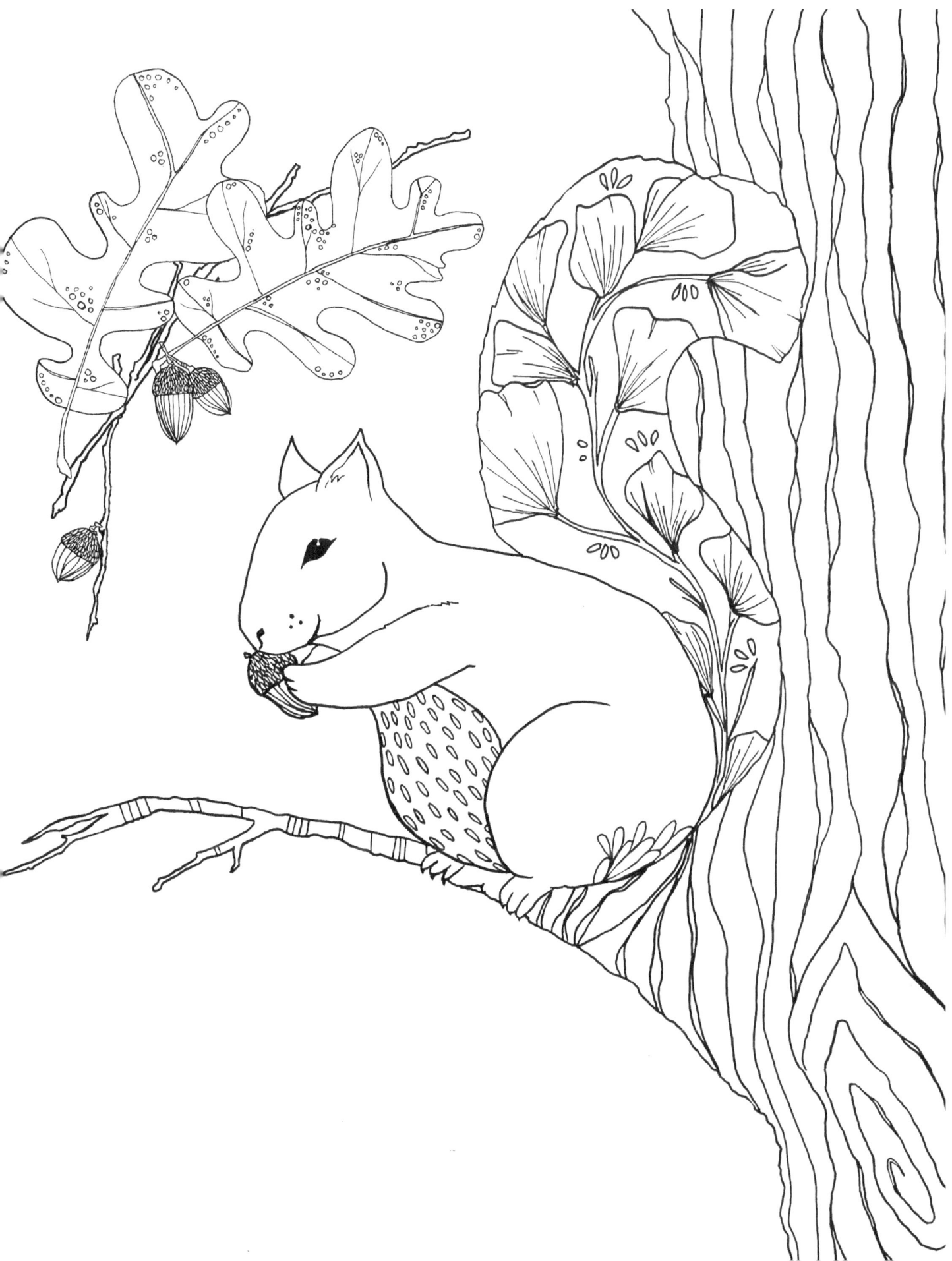

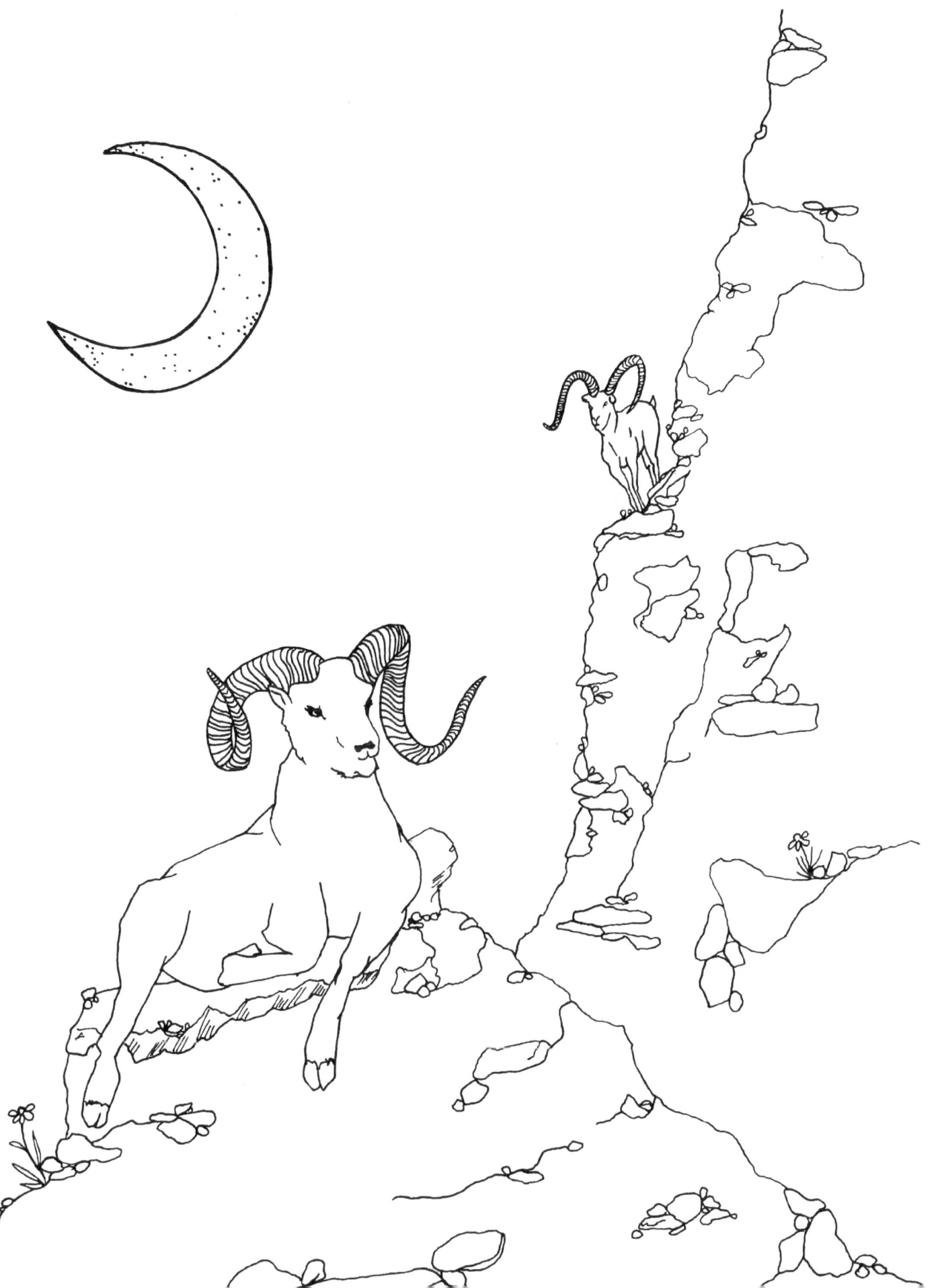

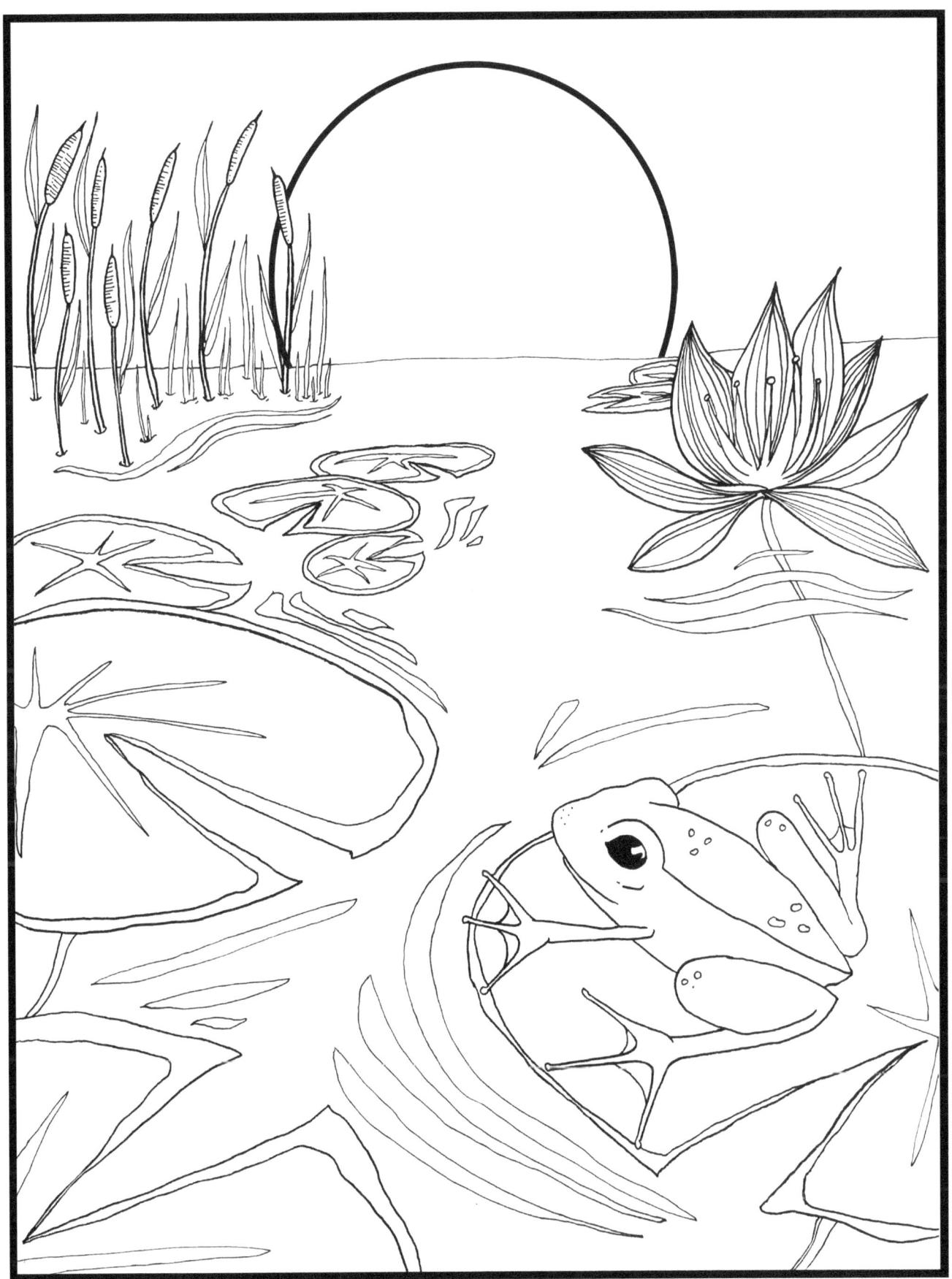

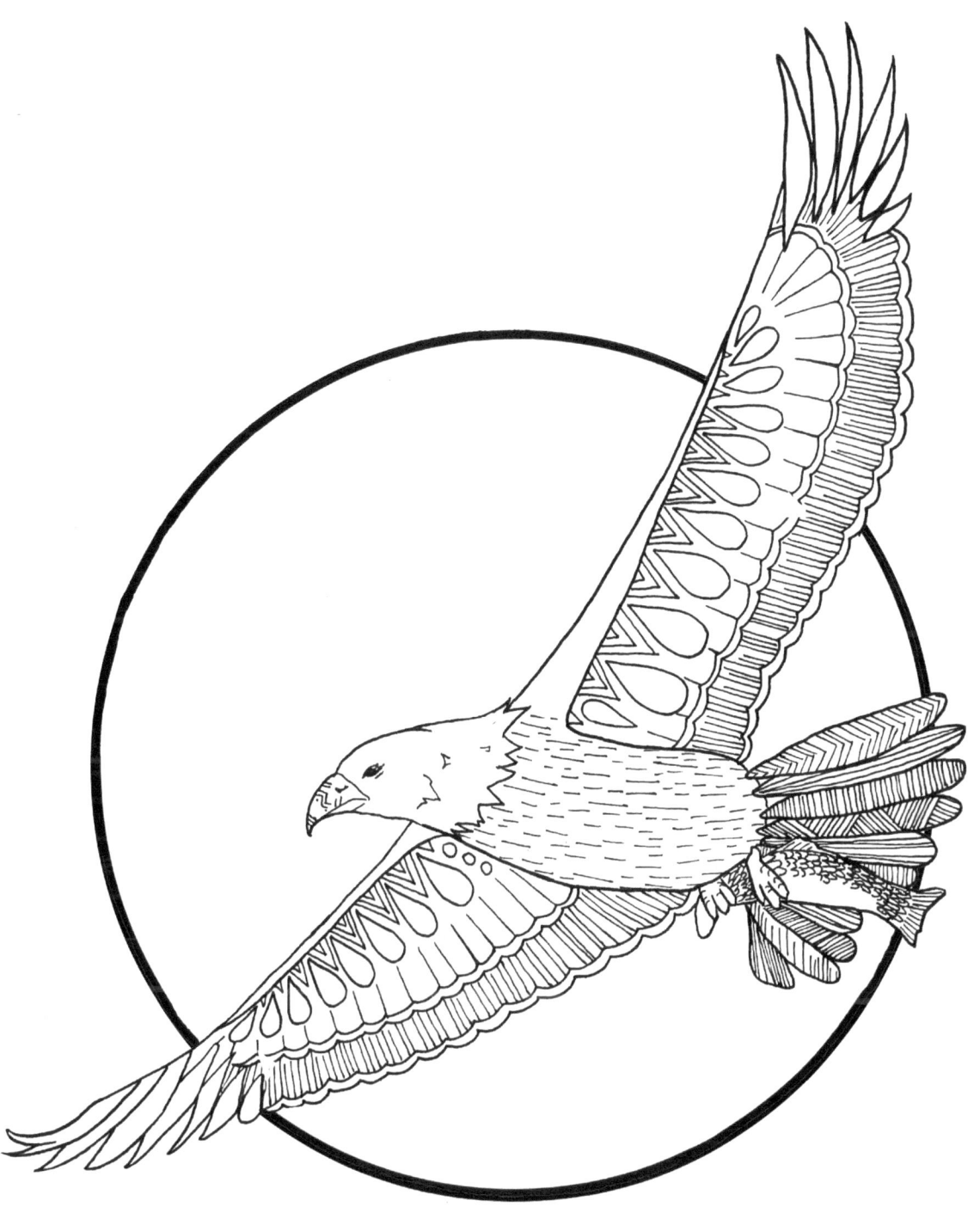

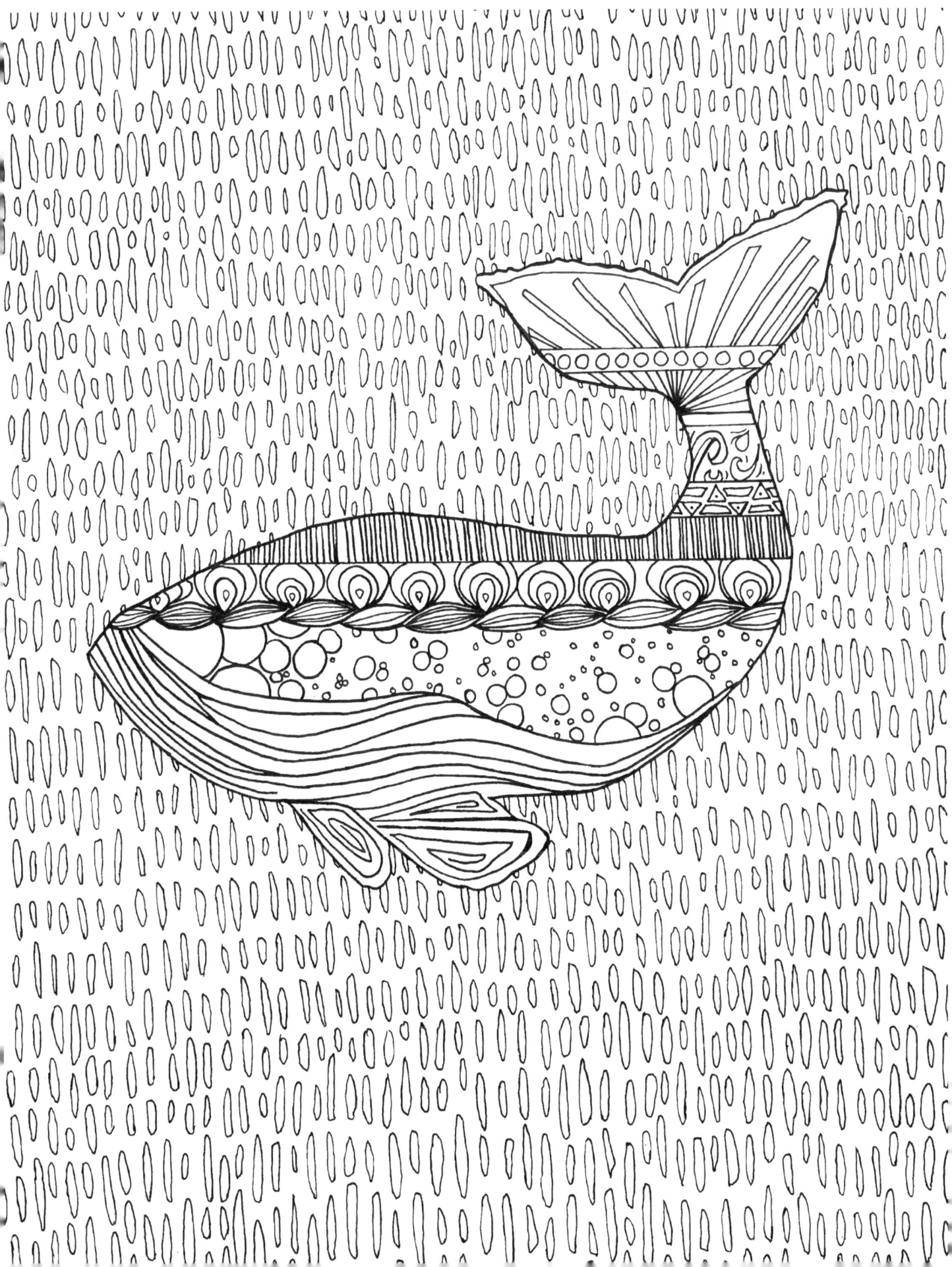

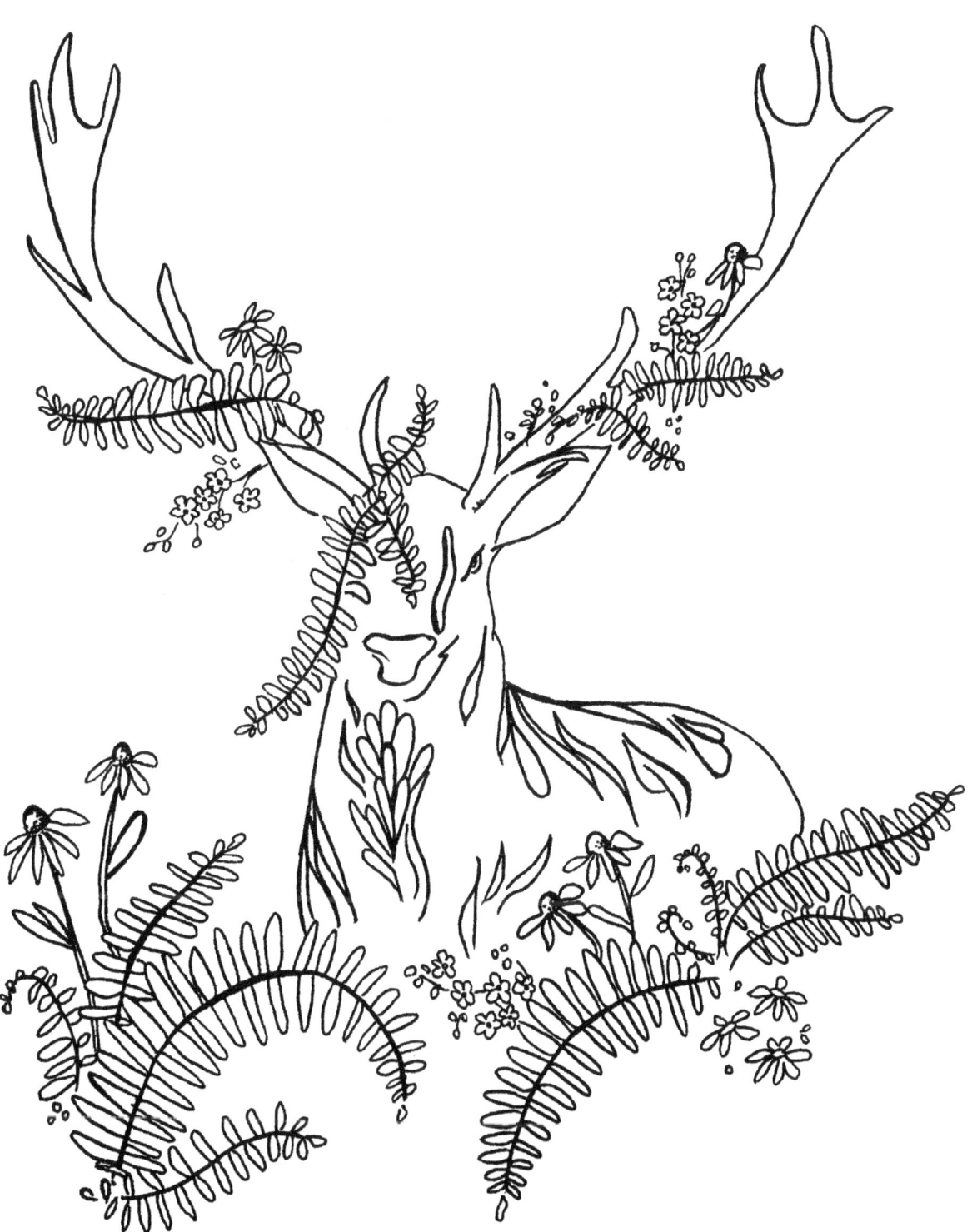

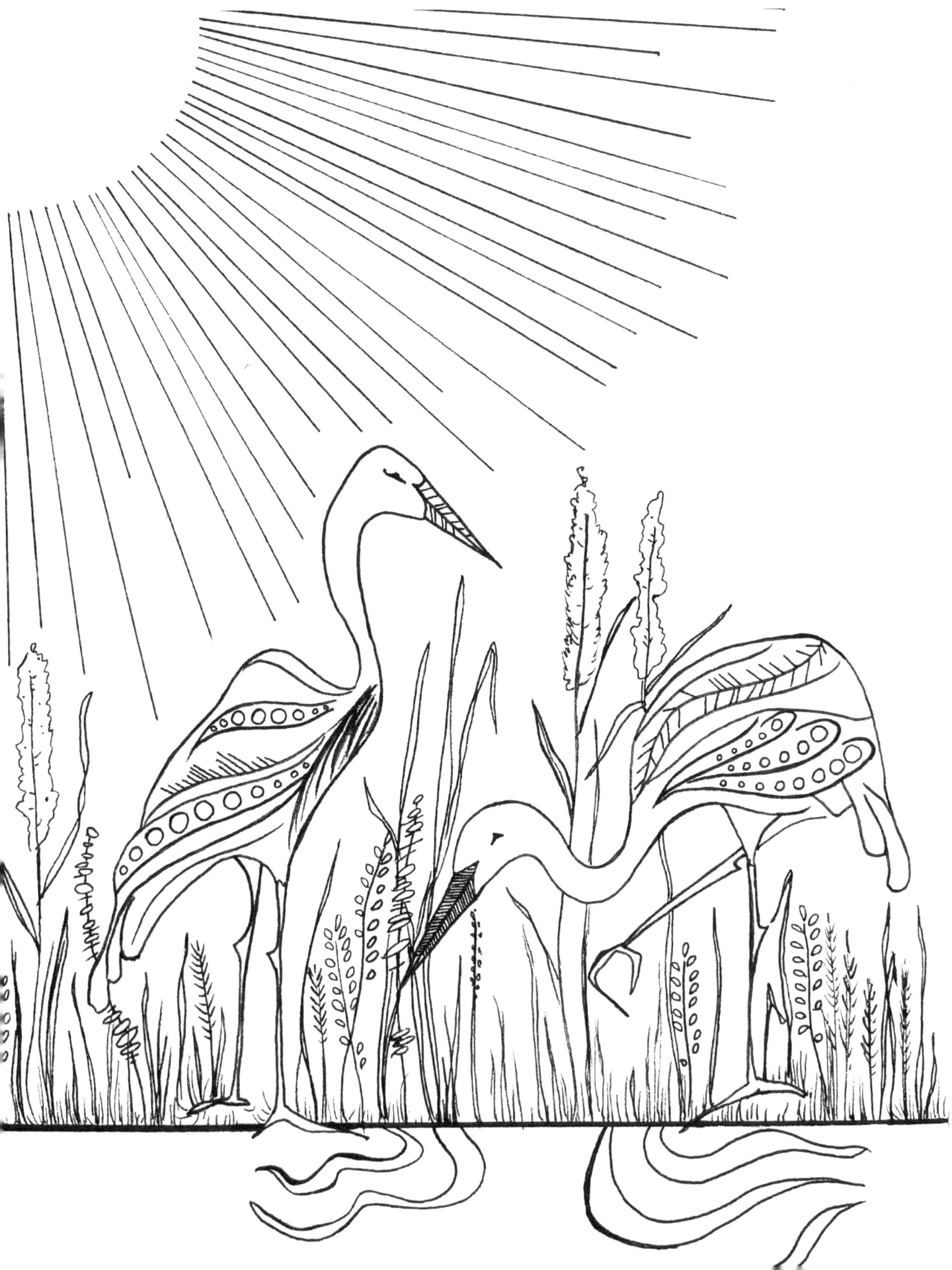

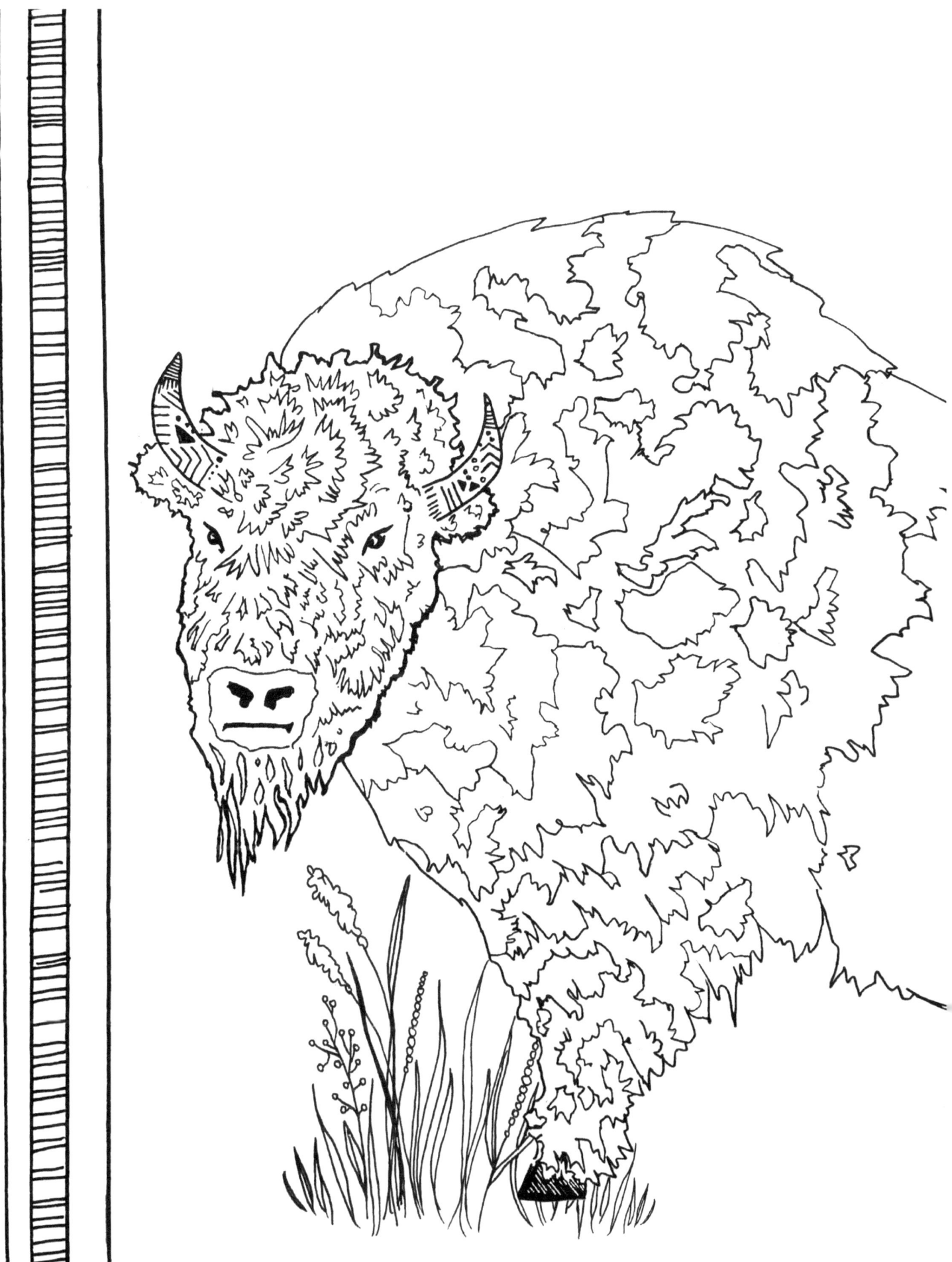

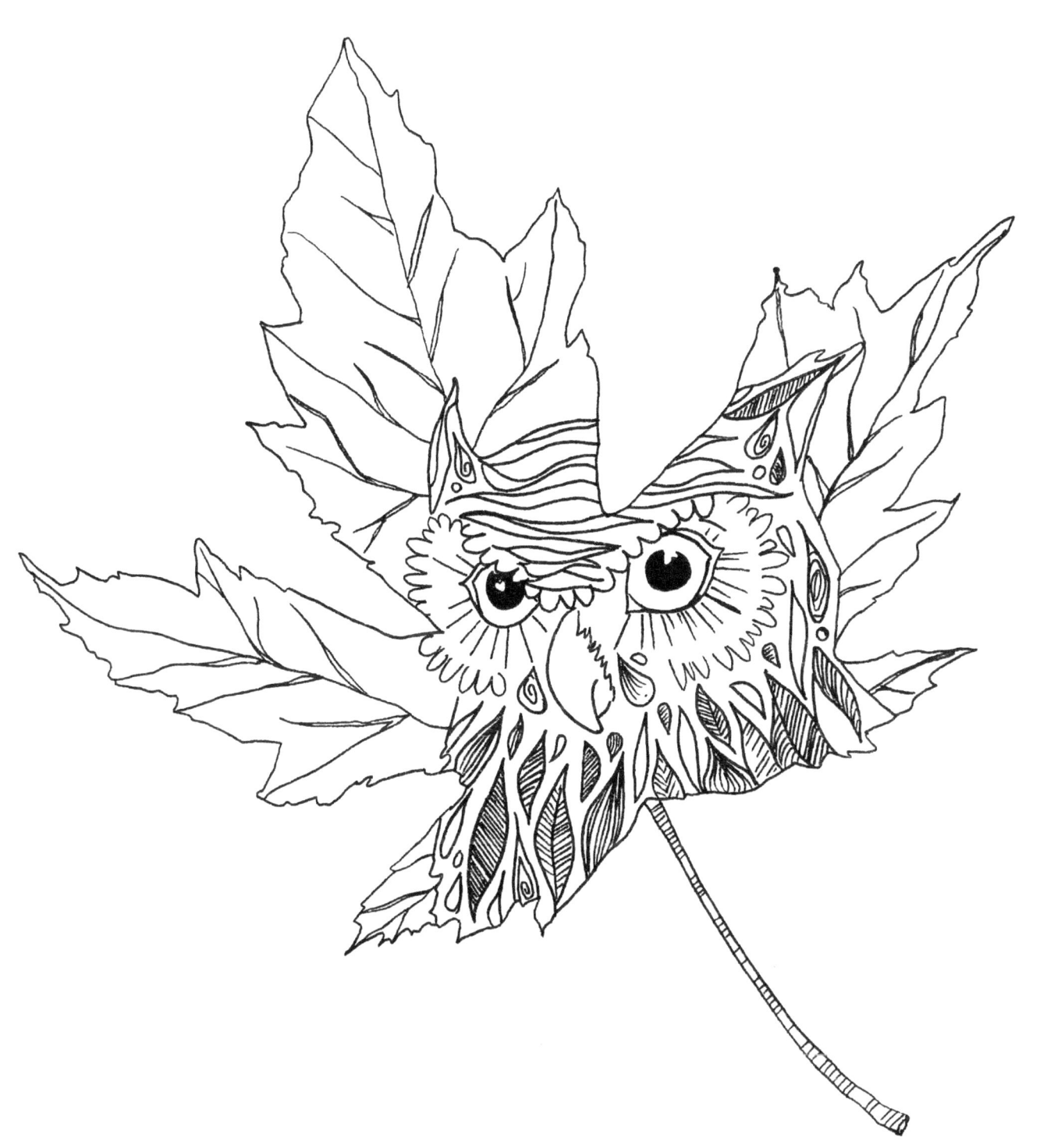

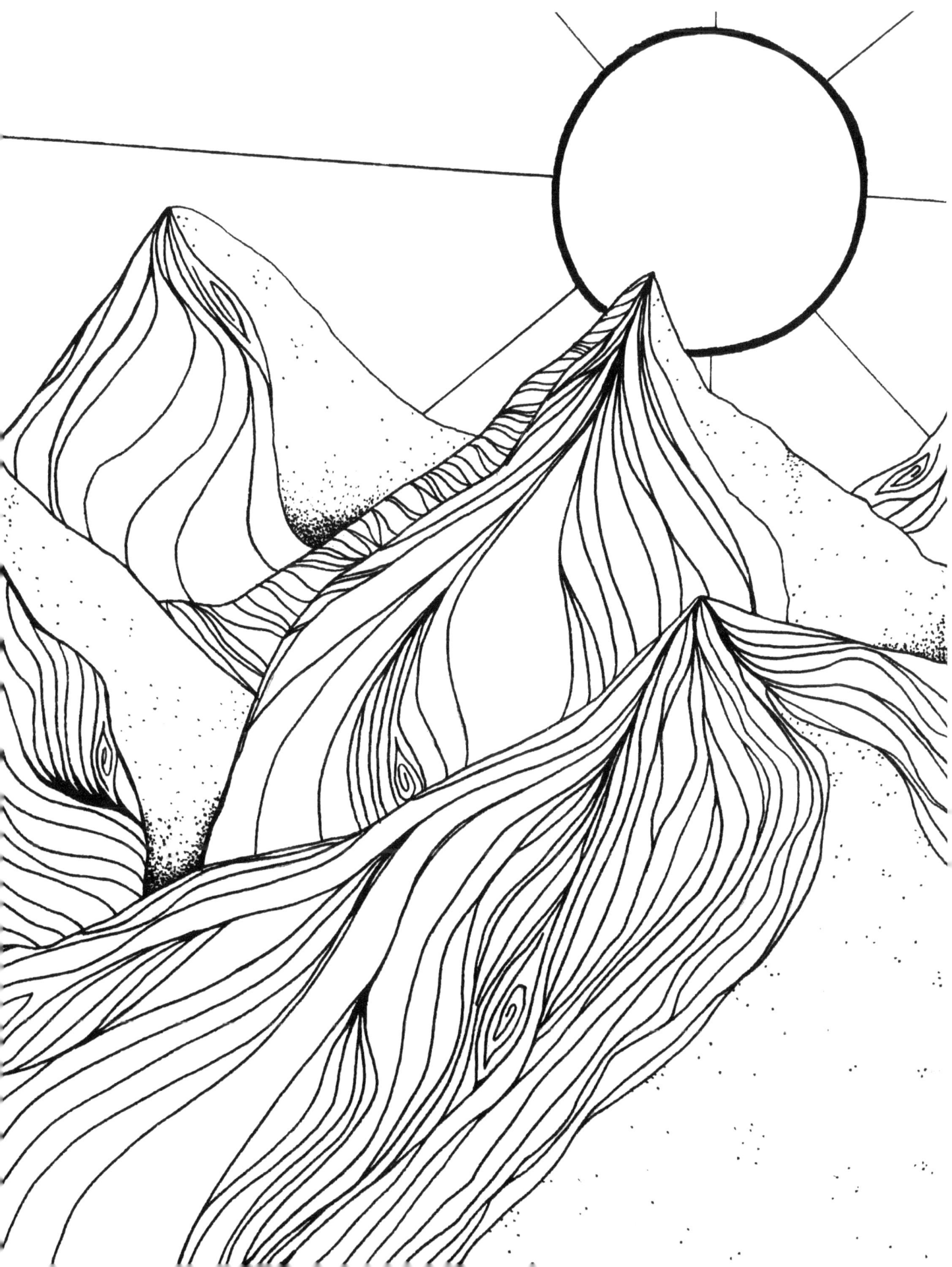

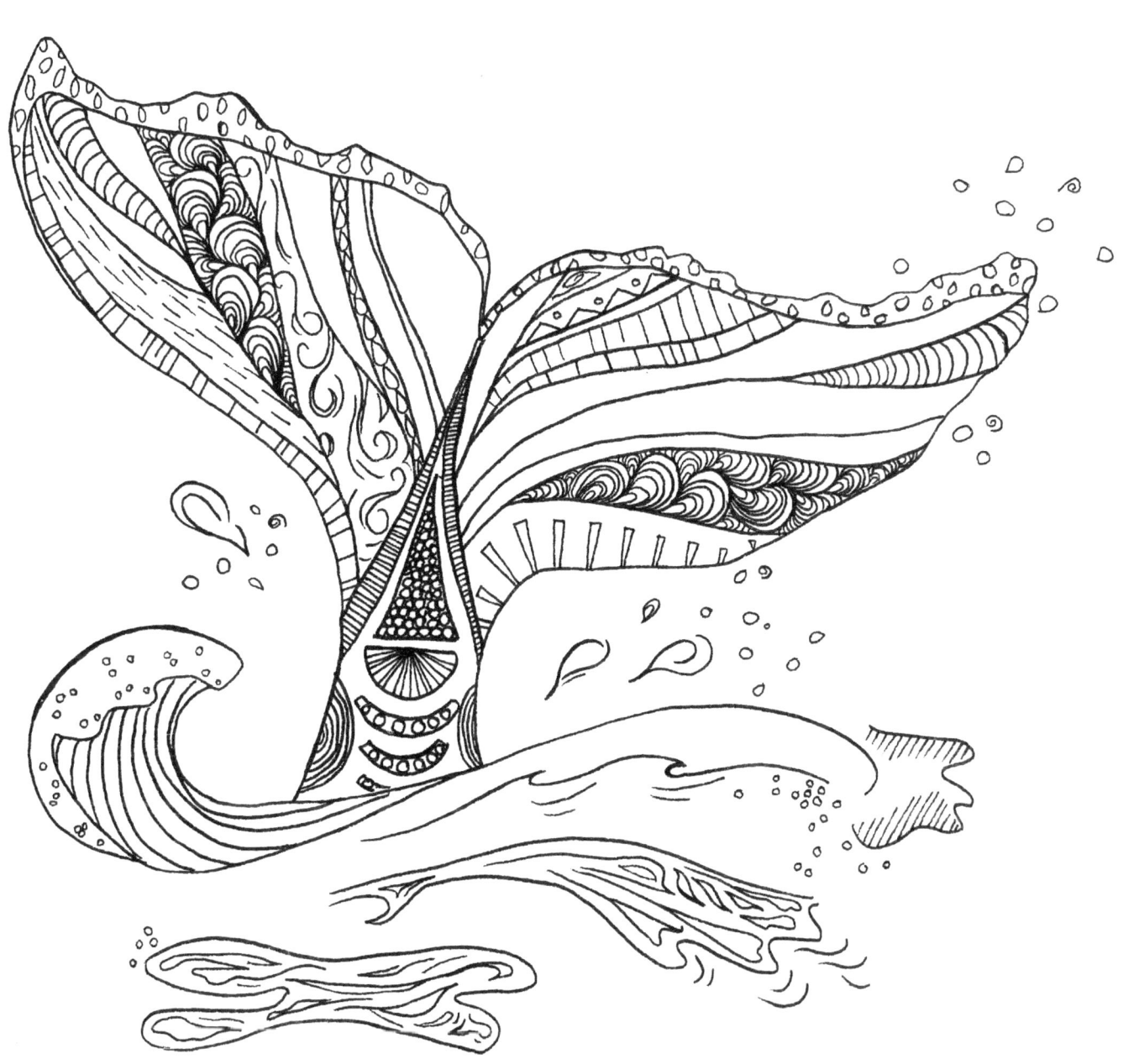

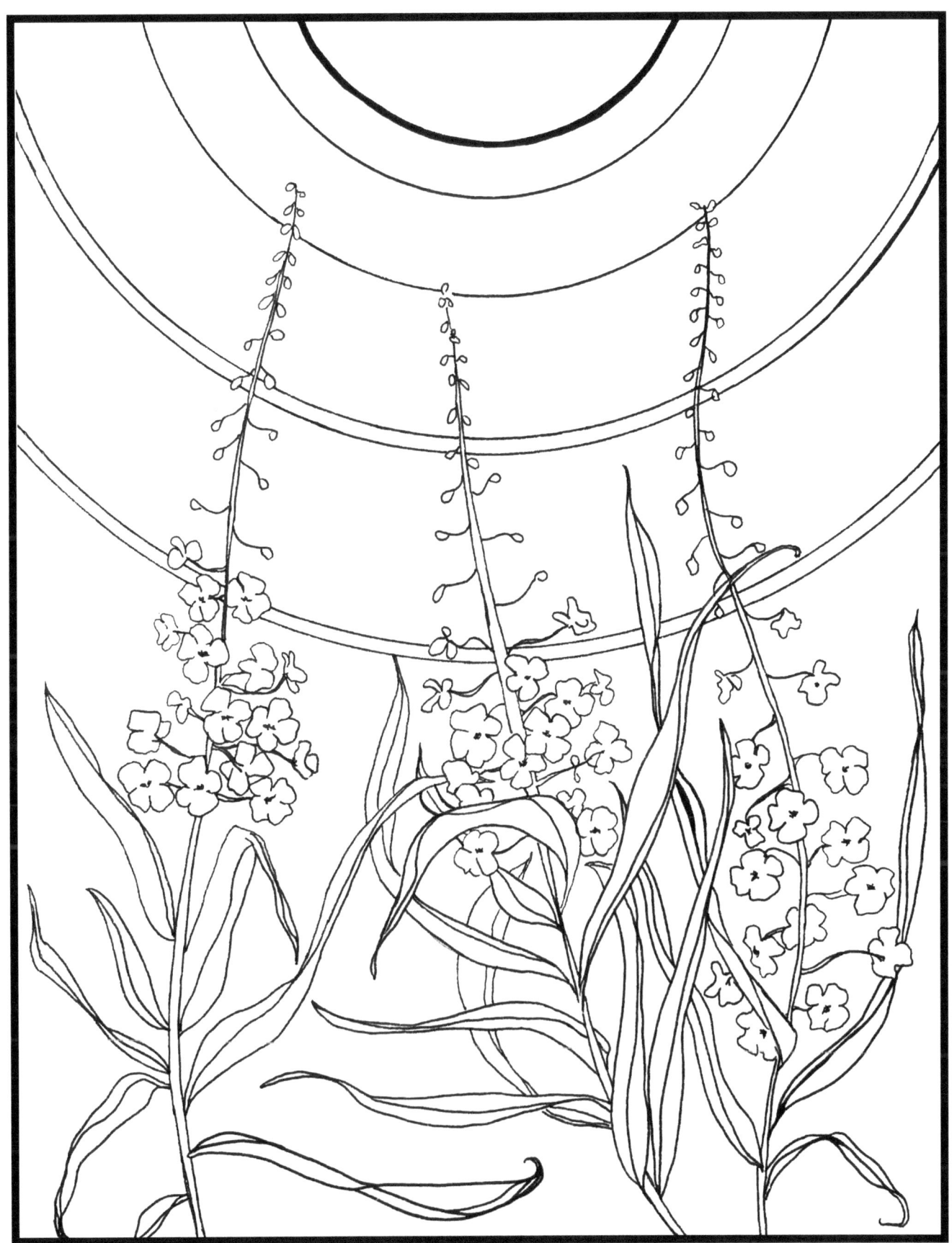

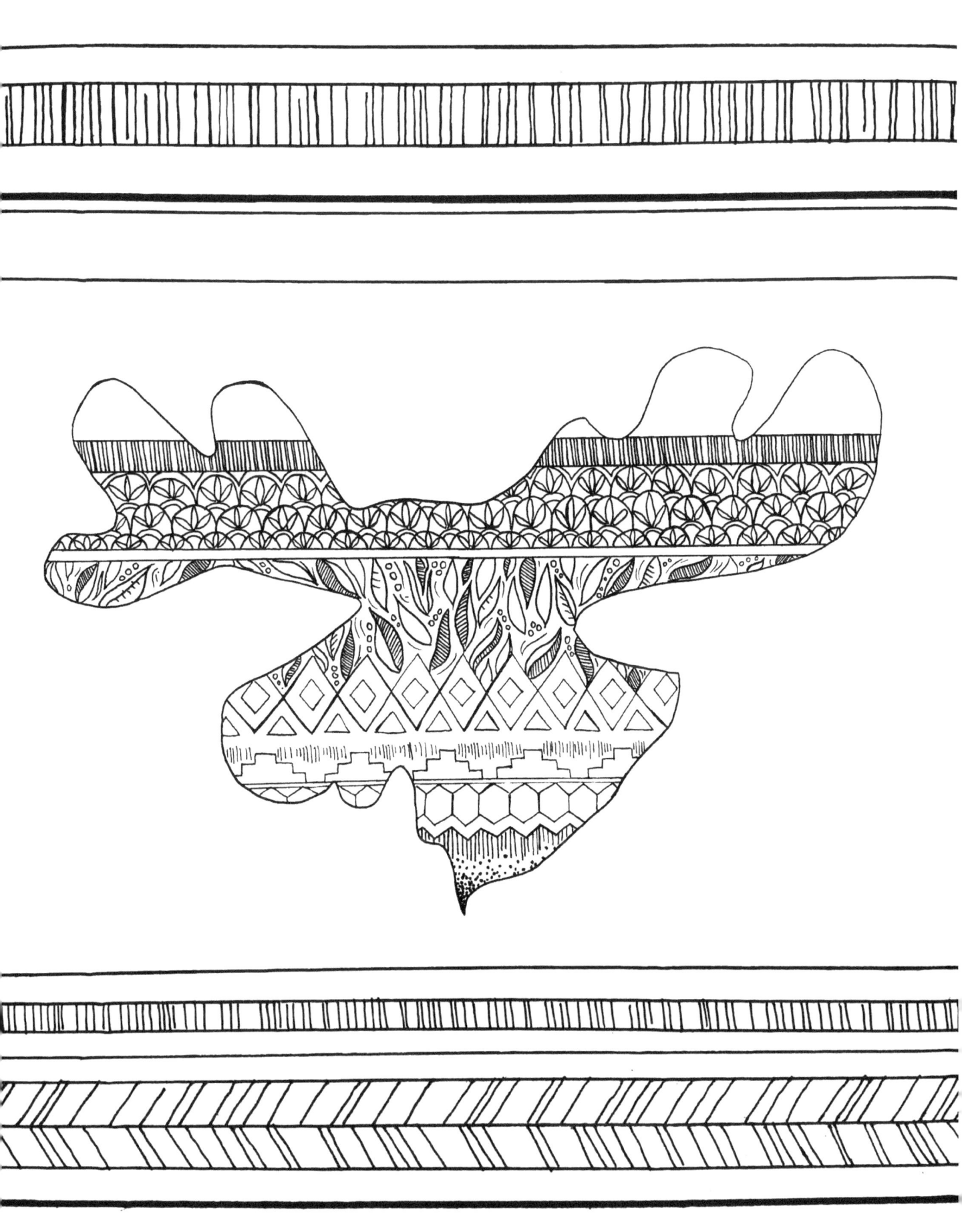

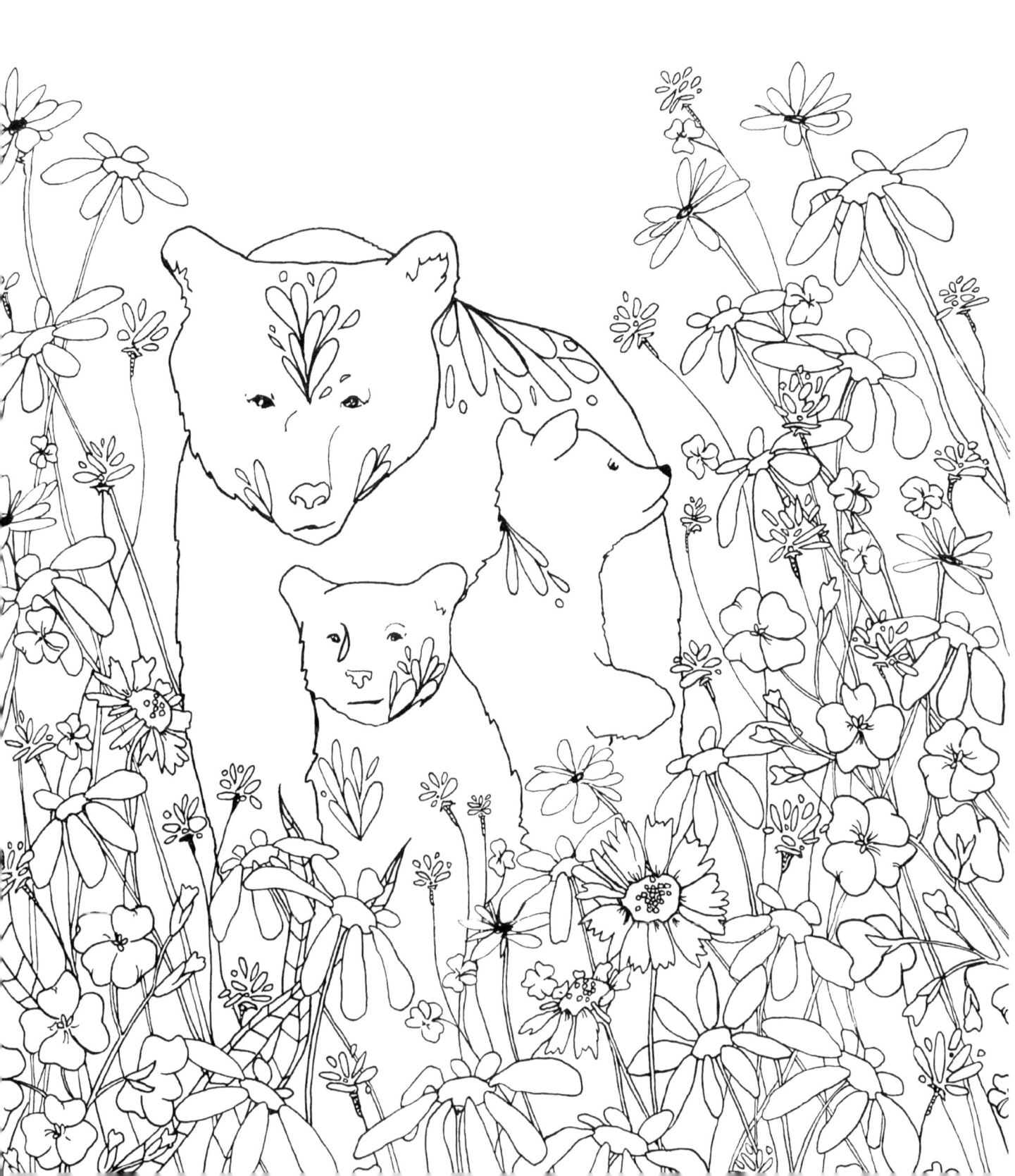

Doodle & Sketch

www.ingramcontent.com/pod-product-compliance
Lightning Source LLC
Chambersburg PA
CBHW040408220526
45473CB00004B/1173